LET'S BE WEIRD TOGETHER

Brooke Barker & Boaz Frankel

WORKMAN PUBLISHING
NEW YORK

Library of Congress Cataloging-in-Publication Data is available

ISBN 978-1-5235-0773-3

Design by Becky Terhune

Workman books are available at special discounts when purchased in bulk
for premiums and sales promotions as well as for fund-raising or educational use.
Special editions or book excerpts can also be created to specification.
For details, contact the Special Sales Director at the address below,
or send an email to specialmarkets@workman.com.

Workman Publishing Company, Inc.
225 Varick Street
New York, NY 10014-4381
workman.com

WORKMAN is a registered trademark of Workman Publishing Co., Inc.

Printed in China
First printing December 2019

10 9 8 7 6 5 4 3 2 1

If you were to personify
the artichoke and the oyster,
they would have a great date.
They would totally get along.

-Parker Posey

Ok this is awkward: We wrote a book about you. We're Brooke and Boaz. We're each a weird half of one weird couple, and we firmly believe that weird couples are the best kind of couple.

Brooke
- didn't eat a banana until age 26
- plans her commute route around interesting garbage

Boaz
- curates a kazoo museum in South Carolina
- former world-record holder for most high fives in an hour

Our editors, Liz and Rachael, think so too, and they asked us if we'd write a book all about weird couples. So last year we started researching quirky historical pairs, surveying couples around the world, and studying animal mating rituals. The more we learned, the more we realized we're definitely not the only weird ones. You, the person holding this book, might even be part of a weird couple. (If you are, blink twice.)

So we hope that you're inspired, touched, and/or weirded out (in a good way) by the lovably strange stories, comics, and historical anecdotes presented in the following pages. We can assure that you that we've only gotten weirder as we've collected everything that we're about to share.

And we want to apologize for this impersonal introduction. We had planned to shrink ourselves and hide here to formally introduce ourselves, but the team of budget scientists we hired to work out the details couldn't do it safely. Sorry about that.

This is a couch

AN INTRODUCTION

Couches are everywhere.

Most people have one or live with one at some point. You might even be reading this book on a couch right now.

And we would all probably agree that most couches are pretty much the same, and there are only so many ways to use them.

When you say to someone "This is my couch" or "I love my sofa," they know just about all there is to know about that.

Love is everywhere too.

Most people fall in love or live with someone they love at some point. You might even be reading this book with someone you're in love with right now.

And, unlike couches, no two relationships have much in common at all. Because, unlike couches, love is weird. People are weird. And when two people are in love, they don't get more normal. They get way, way weirder.

So when you say to someone, "This is my partner" or "I love my girlfriend," they don't even begin to understand.

It would take a whole book to explain how weird two people in love can be. And it's the book you're holding right now.

So sit down on a couch next to the person you love,
flip to any page, and get ready to be weird.

THE AMAZING

The heart knows what it wants,

but sometimes a mysterious crystal ball inside a more mysterious book knows even better.

This is one of those times.

Eggshell: No couple looks exactly like you.
Antique White: Your love will one day inspire an ice cream.
Pearl: You should get a pet and name it Pearl.

LOVE PREDICTOR

After each person places a finger
on one of the scanners, the orb
will change color to reveal
your relationship's fate.

Snow: You would make a great dance team.
Alabaster: You have the best nicknames.
Cream: One of you has weirdly cold hands.

WE GO TOGETHER LIKE...

Step into

A GALLERY OF QUIRKY COUPLES
THROUGHOUT HISTORY please remove
your shoes

Khnumhotep & Niankhkhnum

According to many scholars, Khnumhotep and Niankhkhnum were not only the chief manicurists to ancient Egyptian pharaoh Nyuserre Ini, they were also lovers. Their joint tomb is decorated with elaborate paintings of the two men holding hands, nose nuzzling (a popular form of kissing in ancient Egypt), and doing something that looks like a cross between a hug and a handshake.

Annie Oakley & Frank Butler

Annie Oakley was one of the most famous sharpshooters of her day. Frank Butler was a dog trainer and traveling marksman who faced a teenage Annie in a shoot-out in the late 1800s. Annie won and the two soon married and traveled the country as part of Buffalo Bill's Wild West tour. Annie became the main attraction, while Frank wrote articles and press releases about her impressive feats. Frank died just eighteen days after Annie in 1926.

Marie & Pierre Curie

Brought together by their passion for science, Marie and Pierre got married and together won the 1903 Nobel Prize in Physics for their work related to radiation. After Pierre's death in a carriage accident, Marie continued their research and won another Nobel Prize in Chemistry. In 1911, Marie died from aplastic anemia, which was most likely caused by the many radioactive experiments she conducted. Even today, the Curies' papers and books are too radioactive to handle without protective clothing.

Beatrice & Sidney Webb

United by their love of economics, Beatrice and Sidney were married in 1892 and, naturally, spent their honeymoon researching labor unions in Scotland and Ireland. They collaborated on many books and were part of the small group that founded the London School of Economics.

Emilie du Châtelet & Voltaire

They first discussed science over a meal of chicken fricassee at a local tavern in 1729. Soon after, Emilie invited Voltaire to move into her French country estate. They followed strict schedules and spent each day working on their respective mathematical projects, only pausing for midday breaks to discuss their work and occasionally to entertain friends in the evening.

Theodora & Justinian I

Justinian was the son of peasants and Theodora was the daughter of a bear trainer, but together they became the Emperor and Empress of the Eastern Roman Empire in 527 CE. They worked together to fight off revolts, turn Constantinople into a modern and architecturally impressive city, and pass laws that gave women more rights.

Gertrude Stein & Alice B. Toklas

Though both American, Gertrude and Alice met in France in 1907. While Gertrude wrote acclaimed books, Alice joined the Parisian avant-garde scene. Their home in Paris quickly became the cool hang-out spot for artists and writers of the age including Matisse, Hemingway, and Picasso.

HOW COMFORT

peeing

come on in!

sharing
bank statements

Sharing
Netflix
passwords

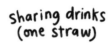

greatPassword

sharing
dreams you
had last night

ok, and then
after your teeth
fell out, what
happened?

sharing drinks
(one straw)

COLD
SPIT
with
bubbles

Sharing drinks
(two straws)

LOVE IN THE WILD

Here we see an ordinary human couple partaking in a courtship ritual at a dining establishment.

The human wearing glasses and the human with remarkable vision consume their daily nutrients while enjoying one another's company.

Here we see the one with glasses remove a tomato from her meal.

She offers the slice of red fruit to her mate, who already has one of his own.

Perhaps the tomato is a token of her affection.

Or perhaps this smile on her face reveals that she simply doesn't like tomatoes.

SPRING is the best time to be in love

Butterflies
Was that your heart or a winged insect fluttering?

Sharing Umbrellas
Being close is as good as being dry.

Baseball Season
Go on a date you won't care if you ever get back from.

Bunnies and marshmallow Peeps
Best enjoyed when just-the-right-amount of stale.

Flowers are Back
Show your love with horti-culture.

TIS THE SNEAZIN Rx

Planting Things
Watch your love and your globe artichokes bloom.

Sharing Non-Prescription Allergy Medicine
Maybe it will work this year.

THE PERKS OF LOVE

free upgrades at the airport thanks to their frequent flier miles

instant excuses for getting out of any situation

Someone to tell you when there's food in your teeth

limitless knowledge of at least one specific subject

which apples do we like?

Someone to remember the things you always forget

a closet full of clothes to "borrow"

I can't believe the Big Chill was filmed here AND there's shrimp!

Yeah it's something

A new hometown to fall in love with

now I need a good playlist for dog-walking

better taste in music

I moved here from Minnesota after m

Minnesoooota,eh?

yep

never having to go on a first date again

4. You wish they would stop, or you ask them to.

who. would. eat. toast. that. way.

Yum yum toast

5. You imagine something horrible happening and how you would feel if you never saw them do that annoying thing again.

um— one slice of toast please

6. You start to sort of love the habit.

Repeat with Step 1.

Lesser-Known
LOVE LANGUAGES

You might have heard of the five love languages (quality time, gifts, words of affirmation, physical touch, and acts of service), but anyone who's been in a relationship long enough knows there are hundreds more.

Pancakes
Balloon animals
Spotting good dogs in the wild
Emojis
Remembering details from stories
Blankets
Disliking cilantro
Competition
Quality silence
Newspapers
Hydration
Board games

Our waiter has the same name as your kindergarten teacher, right?

Contests
Crossword puzzles
Spanish
Libraries
Smells
Trivia
Elaborate homemade meals
Delicious restaurant meals
Grumpiness
Naps
Breakfast cereal advertisements
Skywriting
Hiking
Spectator sports

SUMMER is the best time to be in love

Camping
Like living together but a little more rustic.

Park Walks
Protect each other from frisbees.

Stargazing
Impress each other with your astronomy prowess or your ability to make things up.

Comparing Suntans or Sunburns
wearing sunscreen is also very romantic.

Dandelion Wishes
Don't wish for infinite dandelions.

Berry Picking
Love is in the air and delicious food is on a bush.

Picnics
You, me, and a thousand of our favorite ants.

ANIMALS IN L♥VE

Pufferfish create elaborate
sand patterns to impress mates.

OBJECTS OF AFFECTION

Gifts can be simple or incredibly complicated—either way, they're nicely wrapped reminders of the strangely unique bond that you share. Here are some notable gifts that have been exchanged from ancient times to today in case you need a little inspiration.

Mark Antony gave Coracesium, a scenic beachside town on the Mediterranean, to Cleopatra as a wedding gift in 32 BCE. Coracesium is now a Turkish beach town named Alanya, in case you want to plan a visit.

To celebrate Jay-Z's first Father's Day, Beyoncé gave him a Bombardier Challenger 850. The jet, which costs around 40 million dollars, can seat fifteen and includes a living room, kitchen, bedroom, and two bathrooms.

In 1785, King George IV of England and Maria Fitzherbert, a commoner, were secret lovers and gave each other tiny portraits of their eyes, a discreet gift to commemorate their discreet relationship. The story got out and soon many wealthy Europeans began exchanging similar jewelry.

Shortly after Ulysses S. Grant and Julia Dent began dating, Julia's beloved pet canary died. Ulysses gave her a tiny hand-crafted coffin and quickly arranged a proper funeral for the bird, complete with eight of his fellow officers.

Beginning in the 17th century, Welsh gentlemen would carve wooden spoons and present them to their love interests. Not only would this gesture confirm the suitor's intent to marry the woman, it would also convince her family that he was an awesome wood carver.

Portia de Rossi marked her wife Ellen Degeneres's 60th birthday by creating a foundation in her name to help protect critically endangered wildlife. The Ellen Degeneres Wildlife Fund's first order of business was to build a campus in Rwanda to protect wild gorillas.

Before getting married, poet Elizabeth Barrett wrote a collection of sonnets about her future husband, Robert Browning. Three years after the wedding, Robert finally saw the sonnets and proclaimed them the best sonnets since Shakespeare's. Embarrassed to share such personal poems, Elizabeth later published them but said they were merely translations of existing Portuguese sonnets she had discovered.

Brooches were an incredibly popular gift for lovers to exchange during the Middle Ages in Europe. Not only could they be decorative or even jewel-encrusted, but they were also extremely practical. After all, back then they hadn't invented snaps or zippers, so pin-on brooches were actually necessary when fastening your shawl or tunic or fancy cape.

27

I've always had things to carry, so I've always had bags. Never a <u>nice</u> <u>bag</u> because they don't stay nice for long. I'll rip a strap somehow, or lean on wet paint, or gently set a cup of coffee inside for <u>one</u> <u>second</u> and it will spill.

I just ruin things.

Boaz bought a duffel bag (a nice one) a few years ago.

We had just started dating and we were always funny and patient and full of nothing but good surprises.

It seemed like this could be perfect as long as I didn't mess it up.

30

But everyone has a grumpy day eventually. When I had one, it felt like I'd spilled nail polish on the beautiful new thing we had. Now there would be another scratch, then another.

it's getting broken in

But then Boaz's new bag got scuffed, and I realized we aren't an eight-dollar purse.

We're a <u>nice</u> <u>bag</u>. ♥ All the tiny scrapes make us the way we're supposed to be.

We're going to have this a long time, we hope. ♥

And I don't put cups in bags anymore, not even for <u>one</u> <u>second</u>.

Brain

Dopamine is released, triggering the pleasure center of the brain.

Mouth

The mouth is more likely to burst into song.

Eyes

Studies have proven that pupils dilate when looking at someone you love.

Cheeks

A rush of adrenaline can improve blood flow, which can make someone blush.

Heart

The hormone/neurotransmitter norepinephrine is released and increases the heart rate.

Stomach

Cortisol, a stress-causing hormone, is released, which constricts the blood vessels around the stomach, leading to that "butterflies in your stomach" feeling.

Weird things human bodies do when they're in love

When a person is in love, their brain releases substances and hormones that can have all sorts of crazy (though usually positive) effects. Here's a convenient fact sheet that you can check to see what your body might be up to.

Feet

One may be more likely to experiment with weird dance moves.

33

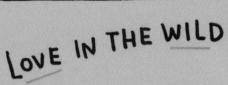

LOVE IN THE WILD

Here we see an ordinary human couple partaking in a courtship ritual on a warm summer day.

As they walk, they hold hands—a symbol of their affection for one another. Their skin begins to seal together in a thick layer of salty sweat.

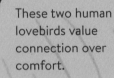

These two human lovebirds value connection over comfort.

It is never too warm
to hold hands.

Never.

Unless sometimes it is.

Quietly and still very much in love,
they wipe their disturbingly sweaty
palms on their outer garments.

Meet Jerry & Ruby

Jerry and Ruby have been together for 61 years, and they're weird together in all the best ways, especially considering they live in a town called Normal, Illinois. They built their house and everything in it themselves and tend a huge garden where they grow all their own fruits and vegetables. They also happen to be Brooke's grandparents.

Boaz: How did you first meet?

Jerry: We met at a ball game, I think. I was with another girl. Ruby was ushering.

Ruby: I was with another date too, and Jerry and his date sat behind us.

Brooke: How did you meet while you were on dates with other people?

Jerry: You don't know Ruby? She talks to everybody.

Ruby: He started talking to my date because they had been in a play together. And the seats were very tight and Jerry had two big coats on his lap, so I offered to put the coats on an empty seat next to me. He called the next night.

Jerry: Well I don't remember calling back that fast.

Brooke: How did you end up building your own house?

Jerry: I didn't have any real construction experience but in grad school we lived in old army barracks, and we could do anything we wanted with them, so we'd put up walls and doors. I set up a new phone line by poking a screwdriver through the wall and pulling the cord through. The walls were so thin.

Ruby: But Jerry rebuilt the place and it was lovely. It was gorgeous.

Jerry: You know we tried to build a house twice. It only worked on our second attempt.

Ruby: Everything went wrong the first time. We had the foundation dug, but then it rained and rained and it filled up like a swimming pool.

Jerry: Then when we were putting up the walls, I split my thumb right open. I couldn't do the work anymore. I took a class before we built the second one.

Boaz: How did you celebrate your 60th anniversary?

Ruby: We went to Branson, Missouri. It was marvelous. We went to the Dolly Parton show. It was a kind of rodeo with a dinner.

Jerry: They served us so much, we took it home and ate it the next two days.

Brooke: Do you have any advice for couples who want to be together for more than 60 years?

Ruby: I think my advice is to always look at the other person as the most valued person in your life, to know that things are always better with the two of you.

Jerry: Some people say the secret is to live more than 60 years.

Ruby: She wants advice on how to be happy all those years though, Jerry.

Jerry: Well. Just enjoy life and one another.

NICKNAMES FROM AROUND THE WORLD

Are you bored of referring to your loved one with a traditional English-language nickname? Maybe it's time to freshen things up and explore the wealth of unique monikers that other languages offer.

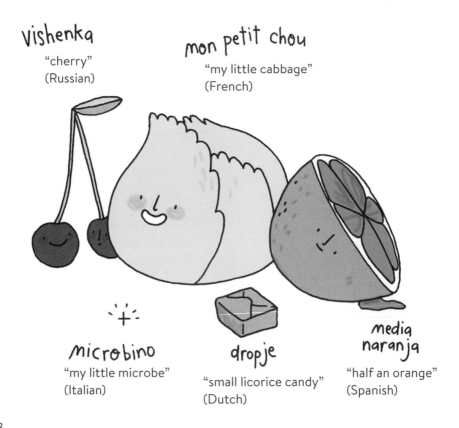

Vishenka
"cherry"
(Russian)

mon petit chou
"my little cabbage"
(French)

microbino
"my little microbe"
(Italian)

dropje
"small licorice candy"
(Dutch)

media naranja
"half an orange"
(Spanish)

chen Yu luo Yan
"diving fish swooping geese"
(Mandarin)

maüsbar
"mouse bear"
(German)

tamago gata no kau
"egg with eyes"
(Japanese)

myszka
"little mouse"
(Polish)

OTHER WAYS TO SAY

bragging
for them

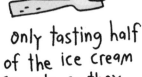
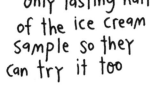

only tasting half
of the ice cream
sample so they
can try it too

actually agreeing
to disagree

looking at all their
childhood photos
with them

THAT YOU LOVE SOMEONE

giving them
the booth side
at the restaurant

laughing at
their jokes

the test
is today?

listening to the
details of a
dream they had

Saying you didn't
want the
last fry

MAKE IT OFFICIAL

Why should states have all the fun? Give your relationship more than just a song by declaring your official beverage, tree, and more.

ANIMALS IN L♥VE

Mice sing ultrasonic mating songs,
forcing air through their larynxes like
whistling tea kettles.

DREAM TRANSLATOR

Did you have a strange dream last night and now you're wondering what it means for the future of your relationship? Here's a helpful guide.

Running Late

At rest, your subconscious mind reveals your heart's deepest desires, and yours are obvious. You and your partner should run a 5k together.

Travel

If the destination was somewhere you'd like to go, you should make it your next trip together. If it wasn't somewhere you want to go, you don't have to.

Losing Teeth

When you were a child, a lost tooth meant the tooth fairy would bring a small windfall, and this dream brings similarly good news: You and your partner are about to get rich.

Party

A loud party-centric dream is your body trying to create enough noise to wake you up. Was the DJ playing a lot of music? You might just be sleeping too much and not spending enough waking hours with the person you love.

Flying

Flying in a dream signifies a feeling of freedom and happiness. People think flying can't last forever, but common swifts can stay in the air for 10 months, so flying forever might be possible if you're creative about it.

Haircut

Dreaming about a haircut is a sign that you're ready for a change. Try giving yourself or your partner a cool nickname, like Disco, and see if it sticks.

Juggling

Juggling in a dream can symbolize life's balance of romantic and career responsibilities. If you managed to juggle them without dropping anything, maybe you're doing fine. If you received payment for your juggling in the dream, you should be really proud of yourself. It is extremely hard to earn money as a professional juggler.

Trading Bodies with Two Mice

This is a less-talked-about dream but an extremely common one. If the mice are human-sized, you crave more honesty with your partner. If the mice are mouse-sized, you should spend next weekend being cozy.

Sports

Sorry, we don't know anything about sports—you're on your own here.

Eating Soup

Many couples dream of eating soup when the room they're sleeping in is too warm or when they're about to buy a car. Is it one of these? Does your partner know you're about to buy a car?

OTHER ANNIVERSARIES

You might remember the day you met or the day you made your relationship official, but that's just the tip of the festive iceberg made of dates and anniversaries you can commemorate.

 hey there friend bear

first nickname

 not mistletoe

first kiss

 **first new food tried together**

 oh no

first dressed alike by accident

 **first time together in bad wifi**

 WORLD'S LARGEST BALL of TWINE

first trip together

this name holds future significance — first heard their name

first sad day for one or both of you

first time one of you embarrassed yourself

my biscuits! — first inside joke

first thing purchased with intent to share

first photo with Bill Murray

CAN FIRST COUSINS GET MARRIED WHERE YOU LIVE?

no, it's illegal.

it depends.*

sure, it's legal!

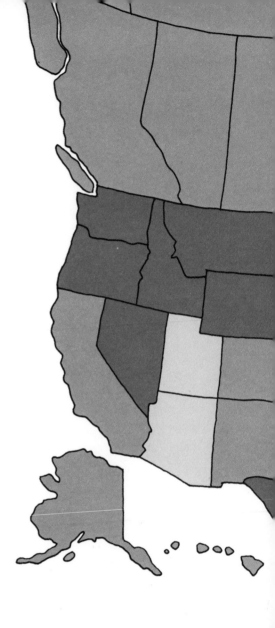

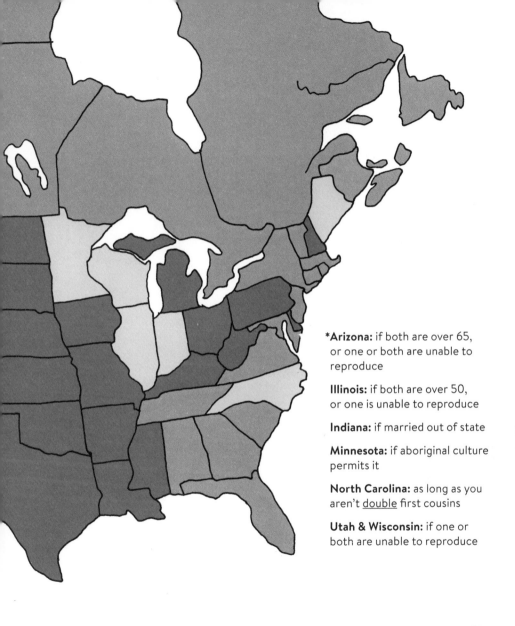

*Arizona: if both are over 65, or one or both are unable to reproduce

Illinois: if both are over 50, or one is unable to reproduce

Indiana: if married out of state

Minnesota: if aboriginal culture permits it

North Carolina: as long as you aren't <u>double</u> first cousins

Utah & Wisconsin: if one or both are unable to reproduce

STRANGE LOVE-RELATED LAWS

Not only are relationships weird, so are some of the laws that govern them.

In Delaware, you can annul a marriage if one or both members of the couple agreed to get married as a dare.

In Monroe, Utah, a dancing couple must be standing far enough away from each other so that witnesses can still clearly see daylight between the couple.

Public kissing is not allowed on Sundays in Hartford, Connecticut.

Montana allows double-proxy weddings, which were created to help military personnel abroad. That means that neither member of the couple needs to be present at their own wedding.

In England, weddings must take place in a "fixed structure," which means no outdoor weddings.

It's illegal to kiss on a train in Wisconsin.

In Salem, Massachusetts, it is illegal for a married couple to sleep naked together in a rented room.

In New Orleans, fortune tellers and palm readers are not able to officiate at weddings.

ANIMALS IN L♥VE

Male satin bowerbirds collect blue items to impress mates.

DOES ABSENCE MAKE THE HEART GROW FONDER?

People say absence makes the heart grow fonder. If that's true, how much time apart is the right amount?

1 new message

If a trip to the bathroom and back makes the heart fonder,

does a whole year away make the heart fondest?

WELCOME BACK!

Some things can make a small amount of time feel like forever,

like new haircuts...

If a car carrying 148 pounds of homework leaves work late and travels 20 mph (how is there traffic right now?) toward an apartment of laundry and a broken sink, how many hours of sleep will you get tonight?

or terrible days...

A. 4
B. 1.5
C. 6 but with nightmares
D. none

or when one of you sees a cute dog outside a grocery store.

I wish you were here, it's just staring inside in the cutest way

So, how did you two meet?

Are you a couple with a boring or embarrassing origin story? Or a perfectly acceptable one that you're just tired of telling? You've come to the right page! Toss a penny or another small object onto the book and choose an exciting new story to tell next time.

An online forum for people who love bubbles.

Your phone numbers got switched, and after weeks of getting each other's texts, you decided to meet in real life.

During a live taping of Oprah you both attended, she stopped the taping to call each of you on stage and introduce you to each other. Then she whispered the most beautiful thing, but you both promised never to repeat it.

You met in a long line at a water park.

You met today, just now.

Both got amnesia on the same day at the same hospital.

Met at a costume party. Both of you had costumes that required electricity, and when the combined usage blew the fuse, you had your first kiss in the ensuing darkness.

Time traveler and medieval knave who begged the time traveler to take him to the future for 24 hours. You fell in love and the rest is history.

One of you found the other's wallet and returned it.

One of you used to be an exterminator who, instead of killing insects, transformed them into humans. The other is a former carpenter ant. But you didn't really get to know each other until you both took a salsa class.

Met on a hike to a haunted cave. You each came with other dates, but left together when the cave's demon turned them both into fruit bats.

One of you never uses pencil erasers, the other always uses them up. Met at work.

LOVE IN THE WILD

These partners have taken an exciting step—they have purchased an Ikea Nörblup, a rite of passage for their species.

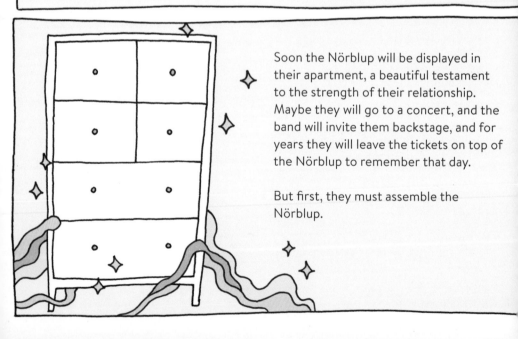

Soon the Nörblup will be displayed in their apartment, a beautiful testament to the strength of their relationship. Maybe they will go to a concert, and the band will invite them backstage, and for years they will leave the tickets on top of the Nörblup to remember that day.

But first, they must assemble the Nörblup.

A task even more difficult than pronouncing its name, which neither has attempted to do yet.

As hours pass, doubts begin to multiply like the tiny screws that keep appearing. Where do these screws go? Were they a part of step 24b?

Will the couple ever own an assembled Nörblup?

NICKNAMES THROUGHOUT HISTORY

According to some scientific studies, using nicknames can be an indicator of a relationship's health (as long as everyone likes the name). Maybe that's why pet names have existed for thousands of years.

900s: DARLING
First used in Old English, *dēorling* referred to someone who was dear to another.

1300s: SWEETHEART
Originating in Middle English as *swete herte*, these two words eventually coupled up to become "sweetheart."

1500s: MOPSY
In England, a "mop" was a fool and apparently adding a "sy" to the end of it made it sound cuter.

1600s: FRISCO
A "frisk" referred to a fast dance move, so this nickname could have referred to someone you'd like to dance with.

1700s: MIO DOLCE AMORE
Napoleon referred to his wife, Josephine, as "Mio Dolce Amore."

1800s: ACUSHLA
This Irish term comes from the Gaelic word *cuisle*, referring to a heartbeat.

1900s: BELOVED
This was one of the most popular ways to address a letter to a lover or partner.

1900s: MY INTENDED
Everyone was getting married in those days so those engaged would all refer to each other this way.

1910s: BABY PRECIOUS
Author Gertrude Stein referred to her partner Alice B. Toklas as "Baby Precious." Alice occasionally called Gertrude "Mr. Cuddle-Wuddle."

1920s: BABY
For a long time, a baby always referred to a small human child, but during the flapper era, it became a popular pet name.

1920s: GOOFO
Zelda referred to F. Scott Fitzgerald as "Goofo" in their early love letters.

1920s/1930s: WICKY POO
Ernest Hemingway referred to Pauline Pfeiffer, his second wife, as "Hash," but he also had a couple of nicknames for his first wife, Hadley Richardson, including "Hash," "Poo," and "Wicky Poo."

1930s: SUGAR
The word *sugar* has been around for hundreds of years, so maybe it was America's growing sweet tooth that contributed to compound nicknames like sugar plum, sugar pie, and others.

1950s: MY STEADY
Sometimes a seemingly unrelated adjective can become a nickname, like this one that refers to the exclusive and undeviating nature of a relationship.

1960s: NUNGEN
Elvis called his wife, Priscilla, by this nickname that he came up with himself.

2000s: PUMSKI
In a TV interview, Michelle Obama revealed that she calls her husband "Pumski."

2000s: BAE
This recent nickname is most likely a shortened version of "babe" or "baby."

WINTER is the best time to be in love

Ice-Skating and other romantic and dangerous sports.

Snowflakes on eyelashes.

Snowball Fights find out or rediscover how competitive you are.

Cuddling Under blankets for warmth.

Cookie Season Show your love with oatmeal and chocolate chips.

Longer Nights = More movies.

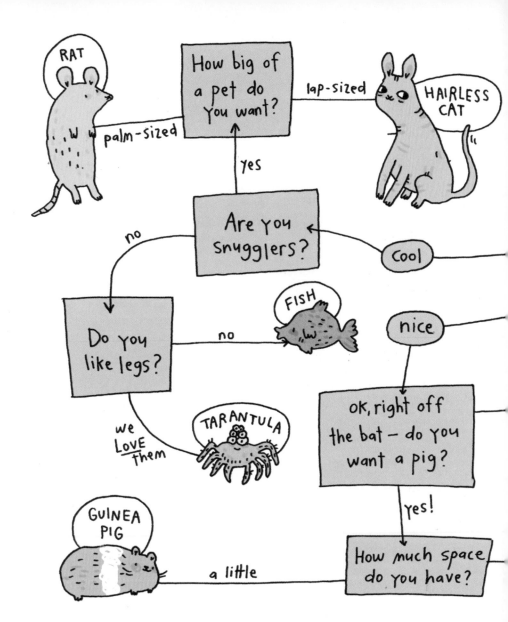

66

A SELECTION OF "OTHER" ROMANTIC DESTNATIONS

Sure, you could go to Paris or Venice or one of those traditionally romantic destinations, or you could choose a more unusual destination for your next couples' getaway.

VOODOO DOUGHNUTS
locations in Oregon, Texas, California, Colorado, and Florida
Sure, you can buy creatively flavored doughnuts here, but you can also have your (legal or non-legal) wedding at most locations of this doughnut shop. They provide the officiant, edible centerpieces, and custom doughnuts that look like the bride and groom.

MUSEUM OF BROKEN RELATIONSHIPS
Zagreb, Croatia
After two Croatian artists broke up, they created a museum to house the leftover ephemera from their relationship. Then they asked their friends to donate their items related to breakups. Now there's an entire museum in Zagreb dedicated to failed relationships. It might not be romantic, but it may prompt some interesting conversations.

THE DRESDEN
Los Angeles, California
Nearly every night for over 30 years, Marty and Elayne Robert have been playing their own unique brand of jazz in the Dresden Room Lounge. So take a seat, order a drink, appreciate the married couple's sparkly sequined outfits, and listen to Elayne sing and play keyboards while Marty accompanies her on the drums (and sometimes upright bass). If you're lucky, they'll play "Stayin' Alive."

LILLE ZOO
Lille, France
As of the writing of this book, there's a fennec fox and mongoose who regularly snuggle together in their shared enclosure at the zoo in Lille.

SAGE GROUSE VIEWING

Grand Teton National Park, Wyoming

Every spring, sage grouse come from near and far to perform an elaborate courtship dance at their breeding ground. Around sunrise, the males spread their tails and inflate their feathery chests repeatedly in one of the fanciest dance moves ever made by a bird.

HERBERT STREET

Dallas, Texas

The story goes that in January of 1930, Bonnie Parker met Clyde Barrow at a mutual friend's house on this street. Reportedly, it was love at first sight and Bonnie and Clyde began orchestrating bank robberies, murders, and jailbreaks until they were killed by police in a Louisiana shoot-out. So take a stroll down Herbert Street and imagine how it might have turned out differently if they had put all that energy into chemistry or astrophysics or jazz dance.

YE OLD MILL

Minnesota State Fair

Climb on a small plywood boat with your loved one and take a ride down a 971-foot-long concrete trough, the oldest Tunnel of Love ride still in existence. It's been operating for more than 100 summers and still takes you past vignettes of brightly painted fairy tales. And if you're hungry afterward, why not sample some of the fair's popular fried foods on a stick?

ST. GEORGE'S CHAPEL, WINDSOR CASTLE

Windsor, England

It's been the site of many royal weddings and is also the final resting spot for King Henry VIII, who became famous for his six marriages (two of which ended in beheadings). Also, Henry launched the English Reformation to more easily get an annulment for one of his marriages.

WHAT'S THE DEAL WITH ANNIVERSARY GIFTS?

Gifts related to anniversaries go back to the Middle Ages when it was apparently traditional for a wealthy husband to present his wife with a silver wreath on their 25th anniversary and a gold wreath on their 50th. For centuries after that, various regional traditions linked certain types of gifts with certain anniversaries. Then in 1937, the American National Retail Jewelers' Association came out with a list that assigned gift categories to nearly every anniversary. We think it's time for an update.

ORIGINAL LIST	OUR NEW & IMPROVED LIST
1st: Paper	Paper bag full of cronuts, rainbow bagels, or another trending baked good
2nd: Cotton	Matching T-shirts commemorating a weird experience you shared
3rd: Leather	Spa visit so your skin doesn't get too leathery
4th: Linen/Silk	Pet hamster and a tiny silk bed for it to sleep in
5th: Wood	Trip to a local theme park where you ride a wooden roller coaster
6th: Iron	Tote bag with the name of your favorite restaurant in iron-on letters
7th: Wool/Copper	Copper phone case
8th: Bronze	Bronzed rock or shell from your first date

9th: Pottery | Mug shaped like your partner's face

10th: Tin | Drone

11th: Steel | Stainless steel slushie maker

12th: Silk | Parachuting lessons

13th: Lace | A ton of lace (honestly it's hard to think of a better gift than this)

14th: Ivory | Donation to an anti-poaching organization in your partner's name

15th: Crystal | Crystal clear vision with the aid of new glasses or Lasik surgery

20th: China | Trip to China (if you already live there, this one is easy)

30th: Pearl | Roomba with custom pearl inlay

40th: Ruby | Aquarium, tiny castle engraved with your names, and a ruby red betta fish

50th: Gold | A wing of a museum named after your partner

75th: Diamond | Flying car with built-in rice maker (this is bound to exist by then)

It's nice to share interests with the one you love. But sometimes it's the things you both _don't_ like that bring you together.

For instance, I don't like swimming.

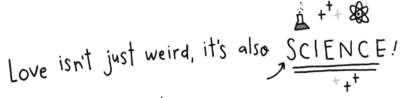

Love isn't just weird, it's also SCIENCE!

Even hydrogen atoms,
the simplest form of matter in the universe,
are more stable when they're paired.

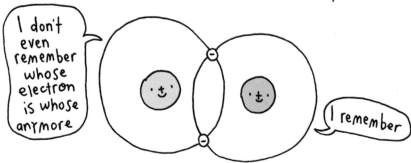

I don't even remember whose electron is whose anymore

I remember

Their electrons want to share an orbital,
and when they do, the total energy state
of the pair is lower than that of
a lone hydrogen atom.

Even atoms like being together.

(Thanks to our friend Dr. Arija Iverson for explaining this to us.)

IT TAKES TWO TO TAN GOATS

RELATIONSHIP

Longest Underwater Kiss

Freiburg, Germany
March 18, 2012
While Nikola Linder held his breath underwater, his wife, Bianka, would breathe in deeply above the water before swimming to Nikola and delivering the air with a kiss. They repeated this mouth-to-mouth breathing/kissing for 20 minutes and 11 seconds.

Most Couples Hugging

Bergamo, Italy
July 3, 2016
A total of 5,730 couples (11,460 individual people) hugged in a 5-kilometer line along the city walls of Bergamo.

World's Longest Kiss

Pattaya, Thailand
February 14, 2013
Ekkachai and Laksana Tiranarat set the most recent record by kissing for 58 hours, 35 minutes, and 58 seconds. They stood the entire time and weren't allowed any breaks for snacks or naps, though they could visit the restroom as long as their lips never separated.

RECORDS

Oldest Couple to Marry

**Eastbourne, England
June 13, 2015**
Doreen Luckie, 91, and George Kirby, 103, married after 27 years together.

Fastest Marathon Run by a Married Couple

**Paris, France
April 9, 2017**
Purity Cherotich Rionoripo and Paul Kipchumba Lonyangata (of Kenya) ran the Schneider Electric Marathon de Paris with a combined time of 4 hours, 27 minutes, and 5 seconds.

Longest Distance Relationship

**March 2015–
March 2016**
NASA astronaut Scott Kelly and NASA public relations officer Amiko Kauderer had been together for five years when Scott blasted off to spend a year on the International Space Station—the longest an American has spent in space. Depending on the rotation of the earth and the movement of the space station, they could have been anywhere between 300 and 8,300 miles apart at any time.

LOVE IN THE WILD

Although this human appears to be alone, they are communicating with their partner via text message.

The missive is sent to a nearby satellite, which sends the message down to their partner. Here we see her typing a thoughtful response. At the end of a long and stressful day, there is nothing more soothing than a text message from her.

But tonight the reply brings no comfort, only confusion.

What could it mean? That they make even the iciest North Pole day feel warm and full of holiday cheer? The human repeats the words out loud, searching for meaning. "I elf you."

Now we see their partner, who meant to text "I love you," quickly typing an explanation. Soon this elvish misunderstanding will feel as far away as the North Pole itself.

LOVE CHARTS

We surveyed 2,000 of our closest friends and asked them some of our weirdest questions. Here are their answers.

What is your partner's name in your phone?

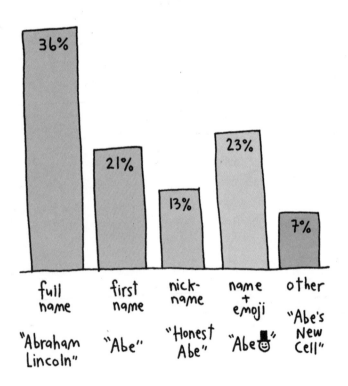

36% — full name — "Abraham Lincoln"

21% — first name — "Abe"

13% — nick-name — "Honest Abe"

23% — name + emoji — "Abe🎩😊"

7% — other — "Abe's New Cell"

When did you and your partner last talk?*

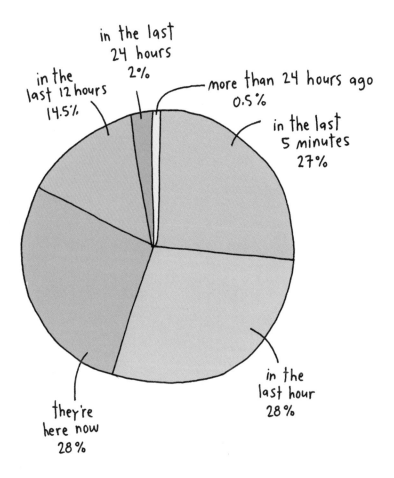

in the last
24 hours
2%

in the
last 12 hours
14.5%

more than 24 hours ago
0.5%

in the last
5 minutes
27%

in the
last hour
28%

they're
here now
28%

* text, email, and postcards count

WHO IS A BETTER SINGER?

Surprisingly, almost 75% of people in a relationship have a better singing voice than their partner does. It defies logic, but maybe being in love just makes you feel like a good singer.

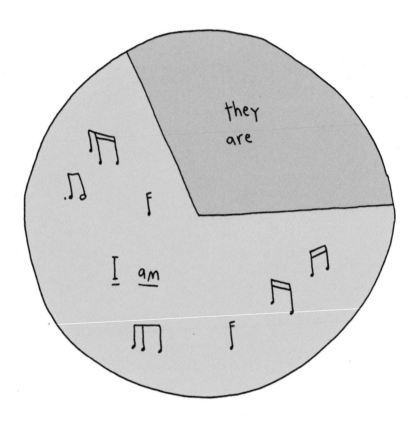

ANIMALS IN L♥VE

Gentoo penguins "propose"
with a pebble.

When you find
a photo of them
as a child

When you make
eye contact while
talking to different
friends at a party

Could you
pass the searup

When you find out
they pronounce a
word differently

When you see
them in the
distance

When they reveal
a secret skill

When they scoot
over and the seat
is still warm

When you notice
an animal that
reminds you
of them

EVEN MORE TIMES

when they
get sick

when you
get sick

when they wait to
watch the next episode
of your show with you

when you see
something you
know they'd love

YOU FALL IN LOVE AGAIN "♥"

when you're alone
and you hear their
favorite song

when you
find a note
they wrote

when you do
something terrifying
together

when you
see them in a
new environment

CAN YOU NOT?

Sometimes being the best partner isn't about the things you do, it's about *not* doing the tiny specific things your partner randomly hates.

Saying "Can I steal this?" instead of "Can I borrow this?"

Loud uninterrupted periods of singing

Spelling mistakes

Finishing sentences

Complicated substitutions
at restaurants

Extensive toe-tapping
or leg-shaking

Talking during movies

Holding hands in a way
that blocks the sidewalk

MOUSE, SWEET PEA, BUTT, SMELLS, POOPEE, SCHATJE, SCHEETJE, BOO

MR, GIRLY, PAXO, NOODLE, PRINCESS, PANCAKE, CINNAMON SUGAR, S

FISHY, MY SUN, DARLING, BAKLAVA, SPÄTZCHEN, CHAT, ALPACA, SQUII

NUGGET, CUKOR, FIREPONY, RUPSJE, POOBOO, WASVEERTJE, CHUM, PUN

GARFIELD, BUBU, APPOLO, BIG BEAR, CRUMBLY PASTRY BEAR, BAE, LOV

MAN, GEKKIE, GRUMP, CHEEKIE, CARINO, SCHATZI, IDIOT, HON

HAGEN, LEMON, BUBBA, MAMACITA, HEFFALUMP, BABY-POPS, FOO

PICKLE, DARLIN', PIRATE, MERMAID, RUPERT, POOPERT, PEACH, LIEVE

NYUSZI, POEPIE SCHEETER, HONEY, POSSUM, LIL DOLPHIN TOOTH, SCHA

JAN, BB ZHUZHU, DUMDUM, BABY, SNOFFLE 1, SNOFFLE 2, POODLE, OO

LOSER, NUGGY, DONUT, BUTTFACE, BUNNY, MUFFIN, MONKEY, BABA, MA

SWEET LAMB, SCHNUU, ANNOYING, HEADACHE, MULI, BUBUL, SWEETPEA

MONSTER, JAM, BREAD, LINSI, EGGI, GOOPI, MAGOO AND GOOPS, BAB

HEDGEHOG, CORRUPTING INFLUENCE, TOK, MORZIBA, MORZIBIZIS, LIN

CUCCIOLINO, PICCOLA, PIE, KINS, LOU LOU CUPCAKE, CA-CAPITAN, PR

BOOGEDY, PANTS, RATBAG, BABY BEAR, BABOO, RIRI, MINI, CHIPS, CHII

FOOP AND LOO, SILLY CHICKEN, NENÉM, PICKLE, OTTER, MAUSE-MANI

CUDDLER, MI AMOR, TROPICAL BEAUTY, JIFFY, LODU, MATOK, LODI, LUL

TESSIE MONKEY, FRISBEE PRINCESS, MRS BANANAS, BEAKFACE, BEEPER,

GRU, MINION, BÜSI, MÄUSCHEN, KÄFERCHEN, TRASH PANDA, SNOOZL

JER BEAR, EM CAKES, POEK, DUMPLING, OWEEN, BUFFEST BABY, EGG, MI

LAWLESS, DUDE, BUDDY, HONEYBUNCH, POPPET, POTATOE, ONION, TREI

KICIA, J. GOOSE, PLATYPUS, PRINCESS PEACH, YOSHINO GUY, KITTEN,

EARTHSHADE, JUCHKA, ZLODEYKA, MOON, LION, SLEEPYDOG, HONE

CAKE, SILLY GOOSE, CHIQUITA, LITTLE CHET, CUTIE POOP, ANTONSKI

BUGSY, BUGS BUNNY, BUGATTI, LITTLE GECKO, PAYSON, DINO, ZAYATS

SQUIRREL, JAY-COB, ARUNY, TEEDY, CHULETO, CHULETA, JIJI-SAN, HANI

LOVE MONSTER, HOFFY, MISSA, BINJA, POEPJE, PUNKERTON, LOVEI

BOLOGNA, CACTUS MAN, MARKLE, PELLY, PEACHY, MACAC, MUNKY, T

JONIPONI. AUG. SKATT, RASSE, JOSSO, TULIP, BABY BALUGA, TEDDY-PIE,

We polled 2,000 of our friends and asked them what they call their partners. This is a selection of their responses.

ABY, BUN, DEAR, BOOB, CUDDLE BUNS, LOVER, LOVEBUG, BABE, JESSY,
TLE MOUSE, CUTYPOO, CUTYPEE, ALIEN, BEB, MY GOOD RICKY, LOVELY,
TY, PIE, MIKI, MINI, SUGARTITS, HONEYBALLS, GATITO, LITTLE APRICOT,
P, MON AMOUR, COCCOLO, STINKER, STINKBUG, LOLLY, BB, POPI, SWEET
FACE, HANDSOME, CUTIE, WIZARD KID, DRAAK, SKAT, BOEBIE, BIGGEST
ETJE, KERSENPITJE, PRINSESJE, SCHATJE PATATJE, BABYBOO, BOOBSIE,
UP, PUP, PUPPY, ROO, CHEEKUMS, ROOBLES, SOFTNESS, SOFTIE, DUCK,
FLEPUS, PUMPKIN PIE, PANDA, HONEY BUNCHES OF OATS, BAMBOO,
FOX, TSIBITSOULA, RAT, SUPER RAT, OWLITTO, OWLITTA, PUPSI, ELIE, JAN
EN, BEAR, CUDDLE MUFFIN, BUG, MASZLAG, TWIG, TWIGGY, BUGGY BOY,
NOSQUI, BEBES, SNOEPIE, CHOU, CHERIE, SWEETIE, J-LO, SO, BABY CAT,
GRUMBLESAUR, GRUMBLER, GRUMBLE BEAR, SNUGGLE BEAR, SNUGGLE
R, POEPIE, PINCHIS, CP, DOUDOU, JU, BUNNY RABBIT, FROG, SQUIRREL,
VE, RABBIT, TURTLE, SMOOTHIE, KUS, DEE, WEASEL, PEAR, SHNOOSHER,
OWS, CUTESIE, FILS, PIKA, PEEP, SNOEZELPOES, SHMOE, SHMOOGEDY,
O, BAE, DORI, DORRITO, LAVA, AMORINO, BABY, BEE, MONKEY, GOATIE,
FRAU, BEBZ, BEBSLINGER, BABE GIRL, POOKIE BEAR, HUNNY, BITANEM,
SAYANG, BB BOO, DIKZAK, PPK, SBB, MEU ANJO, SMOOSH FACE, TOMMY,
BABU, PEBBLE, TOBIN, BABYBOO, ÉLETEM, BAT, MEERKAT, MONKEYFACE,
E, PIÑA QUESUDA, CHIN-ANOOSE, SPRING ROLLS, PUDIM, PANCAKES,
AFT, BEAN, HOT CHEESE, LINDO, DOPEY, RHINO, LADYBUG, ARTICHOKE,
ABE, SQUISH, KITTY, DARLING SUN-SAPPED BLONDNESS, MY MUSE, MISIO,
UP, HONEY BUN, PONELIS, LITTLE MR, PONELÉ, SPATZENBERT, AGRAX
BOOGER BEAR, LITTLE ONE, MIEPSJE, MUSHROOM, CARROT, MUFFIN-
A, LOVE BUG, DUMBASS, KITKAT, CHANCHI, BUBBALICIOUS, BUBBITO,
R FROG, MIKI, GINGER KITTEN, CAPPUCCINO, VIVILATION, SMOOCHIE
AT, SÜßER, SNAZZY BABE, MISS CLEMENT, KOKO, GUAPO, PIQUI, SAPPY
MOC COEUR, TOMSS, SQUISHTOPOTOMUS, SQUISHTOPUS, SUNRAY,
USINESS, MY SWEET OPOSSUM, MÓKUSFÁNK, UMBLI, TAPI, KULIMÁJSZ,
SOME DRIVER INSTRUCTOR, GRUBWORM, BEBO, STERDAM, MEYANOM

LOVE IN THE WILD

One of these cohabiting partners is quietly humming "Jellicle Songs for Jellicle Cats" (from the hit musical *Cats*) to themselves.

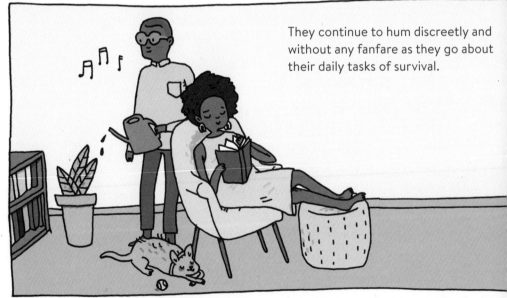

They continue to hum discreetly and without any fanfare as they go about their daily tasks of survival.

The other partner takes no notice as they participate in a leisure activity—reading a bound collection of words while reclining on a soft, cushioned object designed for sitting, eating, and sleeping.

But all of a sudden, the sitting partner begins to hum something to themselves. Are they humming "Jellicle Songs for Jellicle Cats" (from the hit musical *Cats*)? Why would they be humming that?

MAKES BORING THINGS FUN?

Do you love theorems? You're in luck!

So do Bryn and DJ, married mathematicians.
(Bryn also happens to be Brooke's sister.)

Boaz is human,
but a lot of animals
remind me of him.

Sometimes too much.

When he's not with me,
it's hard not to worry that
maybe one of these animals
IS him, transformed into a
pigeon since I saw him last.

Every breath you take
Every move you make
I'll be watching ewe
baaa

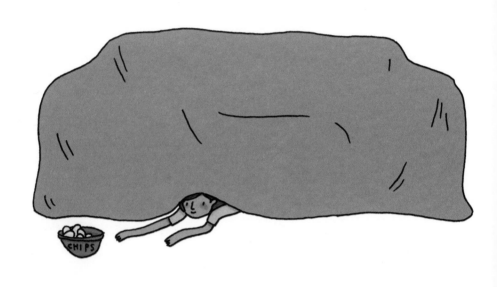

In Conclusion

When we first decided to write this book, we felt a little, well, weird about it.

There are already plenty of books about love, and we're not experts on flowers or romantic songs or poems about chocolate. We don't know if it's best to go to sleep angry or not. We're not even sure if we've been on a date yet.

But we know that a relationship isn't really about flowers or chocolate poems or angry sleeps. It's about finding someone whose weirdness complements your weirdness and creating a whole weird world together. And then trying to say that three times fast.

A lot of people have been in love before, but now that we've written this book, we can say this with confidence: No couple is just like you.

You two are weird. We mean it in the best way.

ACKNOWLEDGMENTS

We'd like to gratefully thank our editors, Rachael Mt. Pleasant and Liz Davis, who helped us come up with the idea for this book and are always so fun to collaborate with. We'd also like to thank Becky Terhune, Rebecca Carlisle, Moira Kerrigan, Emily Weldon, Cindy Lee, Kate Karol, Julie Primavera, and the rest of the wonderful people at Workman Publishing.

Duvall Osteen is still the best agent in the world, and we're honored to be represented by her.

Our newsletter subscribers helped us create all the insightful charts and graphs and also submitted their photos to serve as inspiration for the many couples illustrated in this book. You know who you are, newsletter subscribers!

We couldn't have written this book without Wieden+Kennedy, the ad agency where we met, and Megs Senk, who first told Brooke about Boaz.

We're also grateful to the wood pigeon on our balcony who has been calling to her mate at all hours for the last two years.